ALSO BY ROZ CHAST

ASSUME THE WORST

ASSUME THE WORST

The Graduation Speech You'll Never Hear

Carl Hiaasen

ILLUSTRATED BY
Roz Chast

ALFRED A. KNOPF · NEW YORK
2018

THIS IS A BORZOI BOOK
PUBLISHED BY ALFRED A. KNOPF

www.aaknopf.com

Knopf, Borzoi Books, and the colophon are
registered trademarks of Penguin Random
House LLC.

Library of Congress Control Number: 2018933388

ISBN 978-0-525-65501-5 (hardcover)
ISBN 978-0-525-65502-2 (ebook)

Jacket design by Roz Chast

Manufactured in the United States of America
First Edition

For Quinn,
soaring off to college

Even if you love your job, there's no such thing as a carefree life. Most of you will one day awake in a cold sweat realizing those noisy little people in the bedroom down the hall totally depend on you. They're called

ASSUME THE WORST

~⌒~

This commencement address will never be given, because graduation speakers are supposed to offer encouragement and inspiration.

That's not what you need. You need a warning.

After an uncommonly long career observing and writing about misbehavior,

ASSUME THE WORST

I have one piece of advice as you launch yourselves from college: Assume the worst.

Based on the last six thousand years of human history, it's the only sensible way to proceed. Lowering your expectations will inoculate you against serial disappointments. It will also set you up for heart-lifting surprises on those occasions when someone you meet turns out to be unexpectedly honorable, generous and selfless.

If I were actually standing at a podium, looking out at a sea of young hope-filled faces, I'd begin with a raw appraisal of the real world: It's pretty fucked up.

It was fucked up when I graduated, too, but not this bad. Our vernacular contained no

such terms as "active shooter," "ISIS-inspired"
or "viral cat video."

Still, I'd bet that even the brightest of you
would sit there thinking—as past generations
have—okay, it's *got* to get better.

I'm here to say: No, it doesn't.

And where did you get such a tender idea?

The day I got out of college, in 1974, a vainglorious paranoid was in the White House, shredding the U.S. Constitution for toilet paper. There was a futile and tragic overseas war, hatred and bloodshed in the Middle East, dissent and injustice on the streets of America.

Ring a bell?

The forces of indifference, incompetence and evil—yup, it exists—are thriving in the twenty-first century. No matter what good things you try to do, you're in for a slog.

I'm not saying you shouldn't dream of

making an impact. Just understand that the odds are stacked against you.

One key to meaningful achievement is disregarding the lame platitudes you'll hear in real commencement speeches, group therapy and self-help podcasts:

1. Live each day as if it's your last.

As wise and appealing as this might sound, it's actually terrible advice. If you live every day as if it's your last, you won't accomplish a damn thing. You'll soon run out of money, your car will get repossessed, you'll be evicted from your apartment, and the person you're living with will dump you for somebody with a mid-level management job at BrandsMart.

Spending all your waking hours doing only what feels good is a viable life plan if you're a Labrador retriever, but for humans it's a blueprint for unemployment, divorce and irrelevance.

children. You'll cherish them more than anything and worry about them forever, even when they're all grown up and wiping the applesauce off your bib at the nursing home.

When Charles Darwin laid out his theory

of evolution, he famously concluded that natural selection relies on the "survival of the fittest." Well, the fittest of any advanced species survive mainly because they worry. The nervous caveman who insisted on sleeping near the campfire made it through the night alive. His carefree pal who strung up a hammock in the dark jungle got eaten by the saber-toothed tiger.

That, in a bloody nutshell, is the story of our gene pool.

2. If you set your mind to it, you can be anything you want to be.

Total bullshit. Nobody can be absolutely anything they want to be—no matter how

hard they wish, pray or try. I wanted to play
major-league baseball like Willie Mays but,
unfortunately, I couldn't run, catch or hit
like Willie Mays. And I *tried*. Really hard.
By eighth grade I'd bagged the whole fantasy
and moved on.

Self-delusion is no virtue. Anyone who
tells you the sky's the limit is blowing smoke
up your ass. That's not to say you can't
achieve something remarkable and enduring.
But doing that will be impossible if you fail to
grasp your own strengths and weaknesses.
In other words, work with what you've got.

If Bill Gates had set out to be, say, a
professional bronco rider, he wouldn't have
made it past his first rodeo. He would have

been catapulted from the saddle, stomped

senseless by his horse, and "Microsoft" would

today be a brand of absorbent underwear.

The most successful and productive

people recognize their own talent and find

a way to uncork it. Of course, such keen

self-awareness can cut both ways. Bruce
Springsteen knew he'd be good at writing
songs. Bernie Madoff, on the other hand,
knew he'd be good at embezzling.

Strive to excel at something that won't get
you indicted. Prison sucks.

3. Try to find goodness in everyone you meet.

Another waste of time. Relationships aren't supposed to be reclamation projects. The humane qualities of any new acquaintance should be evident in the first five minutes of conversation—ten minutes, tops.

If it requires the psychological equivalent of a metal detector to locate somebody's true self, then they're not worth the trouble. Life is short. Say good-bye.

None of you in this imaginary throng needs to be told there's a glut of assholes on the loose. You went to school with some of them, and guess what? They'll never change.

If you don't believe me now, send me a text after your ten-year class reunion.

These days we all need a default Asshole-Avoidance mode, to help navigate around people who are intractably arrogant, greedy, conniving or cruel. The ability to sidestep and outwit these random jerks is a necessary skill. If you don't know how, you'd better learn.

Corruption is another dreary fact of life, and the worst scoundrels are often likable and smooth. Try not to fall for their act. From the local zoning board to the halls of Congress, your mistrust will seldom be misplaced.

4. Don't be quick to judge others.

Are you kidding? If you don't learn how to judge others—and judge fast—you'll get metaphorically trampled from now until the day you die.

All of you fictitious future grads were quickly judged before being accepted by this institution, just as you'll be quickly judged in your upcoming job interviews. Your future colleagues will judge you, your future loan officers will judge you and your future spouse's family will judge you. Get used to it, and tune yourselves to judge back.

Sharpen an aptitude for cold-eyed discernment. Selecting friends, lovers and business

partners are important decisions. It's all right to prefer honest, alert, intelligent people.

Stupidity is a real-world pandemic from which there's no refuge, even at college. Each year, on prestigious campuses from coast to coast, no small number of diplomas are handed out to young men and women who barely scraped by.

And that's how they'll conduct their adulthoods, barely scraping by.

Being less than smart doesn't automatically make you stupid. In this era that label should be reserved for those who are doggedly reckless, defiantly uninformed or proactively disconnected.

For instance, you all know people who proudly refuse to accept—despite the tonnage of scientific evidence—that the earth's climate is changing. Arctic ice caps puddle, equatorial oceans rise, subtropical deserts grow hotter,

yet these chowderheads claim it's all a political lie, fake news.

And they'll tell you that while they're standing ankle-deep in tidewater on a street corner in Miami Beach.

During prehistoric times, such blundering specimens would have made an easy supper for the fleet and the fanged. Today, in the absence of feral predators, the unfittest survive longer and cause more damage.

Many of them find their way to voting booths on Election Day. Your duty is to offset the harm they do by making sure that you, too, vote. This will require staying minimally aware of current events, and showing up before the polls close.

When that doesn't happen—when the ignorant outperform the attentive—dimness triumphs. The result is that we end up with dangerously unqualified leaders, and then sit around disconsolately hoping the worst of them will be taken down by scandal, or maybe an exploding prostate.

Such crises can be averted if a majority of you pay attention. It helps to be equipped with actual facts, which are almost never acquired from memes, chat rooms or talk radio.

Society has been deeply divided before, but never has it been so inanely distracted. Don't be shocked if more Americans can

identify all the Kardashian sisters than can

find Serbia on a world map.

It's hard to say whether humankind in

totality is dumber today than it was back

in 1974, but there's no question that more dumb behavior is on wider display.

If I were speaking to a live college audience, I'd have everyone take out their phones and find something breathlessly idiotic that's been posted this morning on Instagram or Facebook. Within moments you'd be sharing video of some drunk shooting a bottle rocket

out of his butt—or possibly a compilation of drunks shooting bottle rockets out of their butts, perhaps set to a chorus of "The Battle Hymn of the Republic."

Darwin would be fascinated by the streaming anthropology of social media. It's a geyser of ominous evidence that our species has begun to de-evolve, receding back to the slime bog from which we first emerged as gasping, bug-eyed salamanders.

So far, our legacy contribution as citizen organisms is mayhem. We're plundering and poisoning the planet with way more gusto than our long-ago ancestors did, while we torment and slaughter one another just as wantonly—and with record body counts.

Technology is all that's changed. We're much more efficient at carnage now. Try your very hardest not to participate.

At this point in my pretend graduation

speech, you'd probably be shifting in your seats and thinking: *Wow. Life is a total shit blizzard, and we're all fucking doomed.*

Yes, life is a shit blizzard. No, you're not all doomed.

Assuming the worst is the best and most promising course. It will keep despair and disillusionment at bay. It will also free you to be pleasantly startled when you get a boss who's actually good at his or her job, meet a politician who can't be bought off by lobbyists, or dine with a twitchy in-law who doesn't hit you up for money.

At such moments, hope is allowed. So is wary idealism.

The profession I chose—journalism—wouldn't exist if young people didn't believe change was possible, even in the most harrowing and soul-sapping of times.

I skipped my own graduation ceremony because the small newspaper that had hired me expected me to show up for work. Then, as now, the only excusable reason for becoming a reporter was to expose things that were wrong and unjust, on the slim chance that somebody in authority might do something about it.

Once in a while they actually did. And it happened just often enough to keep me from seeking another line of work.

Which leads to the part of the commence-

ment address when every speaker feels

obliged to talk about happiness. Where do you

find it? How do you sustain it?

I haven't got a clue. If you're searching for

a spiritual pathway to serenity, ask your yoga teacher. Or maybe buy a puppy.

Here's all I know about happiness: It's slippery. It's unpredictable. It's a different sensation for everyone.

But one thing happiness is *not* is overrated. When you luck into some, enjoy every minute.

Grandparents of my generation were fond of telling us to "spread a little happiness wherever you go." For some of you it will be easier to spread the flu.

Happiness can't be sprinkled around like fairy dust. By disposition some folks are more contented than others, but none of us glides along in a cloud of perpetual bliss.

People who are truly hurting are grateful for one happy moment. All it takes to bring them a smile—or maybe a laugh—is a single act of comfort.

For many of you, reaching out to help will be a moral reflex. To those who must be reminded to behave that way, let me say this: Your parents dropped the ball, big-time. Force yourself to experiment with kindness, even when the impulse eludes you.

If I were speaking to actual graduates, I could look out over the crowd and predict

with absolute certainty that some of you
are blessed with monster talent, and you'll
do amazing things. You won't change the
whole world, but you'll change *somebody's*
world—and for the better.

And, just as inevitably, some of you won't.
You'll park your principles in the long-term
lot and spend your future taking advantage of
people. Others of you, burdened with a deficit
of ambition, won't do much of anything.
You could easily end up working in a robocall
center, peddling shitty insurance policies to
senior citizens.

At the other end of the productivity
spectrum, those of you who own a func-
tioning conscience, a sturdy set of values and

a tolerance for hard work ought to do just
fine. You deserve many happy moments.

If you set your mind to it, you can be
lots of things, but not the next Willie Mays,
a champion bronco rider or even an acoustic
shadow of Bruce Springsteen.

To sum up:

Figure out what you're good at, and get better at it. Along the way, don't waste your time on people whose decency isn't apparent when you first meet for a cup of coffee. Be an astute judge of character, and learn to judge quickly.

Read the news. Pay attention. Always aspire to act in a way that cancels out someone else's cruel or stupid behavior.

Never stop worrying. Live each day as if your rent is due tomorrow.

And always, *always* be the one who sleeps near the campfire—the one who would make Darwin proud.

~~~

A NOTE ABOUT THE AUTHOR

CARL HIAASEN was born and raised in
Florida. He is the author of fourteen novels,
including the best sellers *Razor Girl*, *Bad
Monkey*, *Star Island*, *Nature Girl*, *Skinny
Dip*, *Sick Puppy* and *Lucky You*, and five
best-selling children's books: *Hoot*, *Flush*,
Scat, *Chomp* and *Skink*. His most recent
work of nonfiction is *Dance of the Reptiles*,
a collection of his columns from *The
Miami Herald*.

A NOTE ABOUT THE ILLUSTRATOR

ROZ CHAST grew up in Brooklyn. In 1978, her cartoons began appearing in *The New Yorker,* where she has since published more than one thousand. She wrote and illustrated, most recently, *Going into Town;* the number one *New York Times* best seller *Can't We Talk About Something More Pleasant?,* a National Book Critics Circle Award and Kirkus Prize winner and a finalist for the National Book Award; *What I Hate: From A to Z;* and her cartoon collections *Theories of Everything* and *The Party, After You Left.*

A NOTE ON THE TYPE

This book was set in Scala, a typeface designed by the Dutch designer Martin Majoor (b. 1960) in 1988 and released by the FontFont foundry in 1990. While designed as a fully modern family of fonts containing both a serif and a sans serif alphabet, Scala retains many refinements normally associated with traditional fonts.

Composed by North Market Street Graphics, Lancaster, Pennsylvania.
Printed and bound by Thomson-Shore, Dexter, Michigan.
Designed by Peter A. Andersen.